HORSES

The
AMERICAN PAINT
Horse

by David Denniston

Consultant:
Jerry Circelli
Director of Communications
American Paint Horse Association (APHA)
Fort Worth, Texas

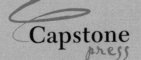

Capstone
press

Mankato, Minnesota

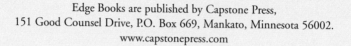

Edge Books are published by Capstone Press,
151 Good Counsel Drive, P.O. Box 669, Mankato, Minnesota 56002.
www.capstonepress.com

Library of Congress Cataloging-in-Publication Data
Denniston, David.
    The American paint horse / by David Denniston.
    p. cm.—(Edge books. Horses)
    Includes bibliographical references (p. 31) and index.
    ISBN 0-7368-3763-9 (hardcover)
    1. American paint horse—Juvenile literature. I. Title. II. Series.
SF293.A47D46 2005
636.1'3—dc22
                                                                2004019414

Summary: Describes the American Paint Horse, including its history, physical features, and uses today.

Editorial Credits
Carrie A. Braulick, editor; Juliette Peters, designer; Deirdre Barton,
    photo researcher; Scott Thoms, photo editor

Photo Credits
APHA Photos, 9, 25; Jerry Circelli, 7
Capstone Press/Gary Sundermeyer, 6, 14, 22
Gary Langston/Strawberry River Photography and Film Company, 5
Mark J. Barrett, front cover, back cover, 11, 12, 13, 16–17, 29
Photo by Charles Hilton, 23
Prophoto by Lori, 15, 19, 20
Sharon P. Fibelkorn, 26

1 2 3 4 5 6 10 09 08 07 06 05

Table of Contents

Chapter 1

An American Horse

Hundreds of years ago, early relatives of the American Paint Horse roamed the North American landscape. American Indians liked the horses for their color and calm personalities. Soon, early U.S. settlers rode the spotted horses on ranches. The horses' eye-catching spots also made them popular in early U.S. Western shows.

Today, Paints are a symbol of American history. Paints remind people of a time when the country's borders first began stretching from sea to sea.

Learn about:
* Hernán Cortés
* Paints in rodeos
* Rebecca Tyler Lockhart

American Indians have a long history of working with Paint horses.

Early Relatives of Paints

In 1519, explorer Hernán Cortés sailed from Spain to Mexico. Cortés wanted to find gold and claim land for Spain. Cortés brought 16 horses with him. One of these horses was brown with white spots.

Soon, English, French, and other European explorers brought horses to North America. The spotted horse mated with these horses. Many of the spotted horse's offspring also had spots. These horses were early relatives of today's Paints.

Paints and American Indians

Some American Indians rode horses to help them hunt buffalo. They especially liked the spotted horses. The horses blended with the surroundings. This camouflage coloring helped Indians sneak up on buffalo. It also helped them hide from enemies during battles. Some American Indians believed the spotted horses had magical powers.

Paints as Movie Stars

In 2004, the movie *Hidalgo* was released. *Hidalgo* is based on a famous legend. According to the story, endurance rider Frank T. Hopkins entered his Spanish Mustang, Hidalgo, in a 3,000-mile (4,828-kilometer) race in 1889. Few people thought Hopkins would win. Arabian horses are known as the best endurance racers. Yet Hopkins won the race on Hidalgo.

Five Paints played the role of Hidalgo. These horses had similar color patterns. *Hidalgo's* cast and crew liked the horses. Screenwriter John Fusco and actor Viggo Mortensen each bought a Paint that starred in the movie.

Paints in the West

By the mid-1800s, European settlers controlled much of the land where American Indians once lived. Many settlers in the western United States lived on large cattle ranches. The ranchers rode horses to help them herd cattle. They called spotted horses "Paints."

In the early 1900s, the sport of rodeo became popular in the United States. Cowboys competed in several events related to ranching. Many rodeo riders impressed crowds on their fast, athletic Paints.

The APHA

By the late 1950s, Paint owners wanted to form a breed registry to keep track of each Paint's ancestry. In 1962, Rebecca Tyler Lockhart and other Paint owners started the American Paint Stock Horse Association. The name was later changed to the American Paint Horse Association (APHA).

Today, about 800,000 horses are registered with the APHA. It is the second largest U.S. horse breed registry.

▲ Some people still use Paints on ranches.

Chapter 2

A Horse of Many Colors

The color patterns of Paints are their best-known feature. People often mate Paints with horses of other breeds and hope the foals will have the Paint's famous spots. But the Paint's color is only one of its admired features. Paints also are known for their calmness, strength, and speed.

Coloring

To be registered by the APHA, a Paint must have at least one spot. Many Paints have white spots on a dark coat color. Other Paints have dark spots on a white body.

A Paint's coat can be almost any color. Black, bay, brown, buckskin, and chestnut are common.

Learn about:
- ★ **Main coat patterns**
- ★ **Body frame**
- ★ **Personality**

Most Paints have several white spots. Some Paints are almost completely white.

Tobiano Paints often have dark heads and white leg markings.

Bay horses are a shade of red-brown. They usually have black manes and tails. Buckskin Paints are tan, and chestnut horses are a copper color.

Coat Patterns

Paints have three main coat patterns. These patterns are the tobiano, overo, and tovero.

The tobiano pattern is the most common. The tobiano's spots often are rounded. White hair is common on all legs. Dark hair usually covers the flanks, or the fleshy area in front of the back legs. The tobiano's head often is dark.

The overo Paint usually has dark hair across its back. The overo's spots often appear scattered or splashy. Dark coloring is common on at least one leg.

▼ Overo Paints usually have dark coloring that crosses the back. Spots are often scattered.

13

The tovero is a mix of the overo and tobiano patterns. Many toveros have dark hair around the ears. Often, one or both eyes are blue.

Main Features

The Paint is a stock horse. A stock horse has a large frame and a muscular body. To be registered, each Paint must have parents that are registered as Paints, Quarter Horses, or Thoroughbreds. These horse breeds also are stock horses.

The Paint's stock horse features are easy to recognize. It has a broad chest that leads to a finely muscled neck. The horse's strong legs and muscular hindquarters help it pick up speed quickly.

The height of a horse is measured from the ground to the withers, or top of the shoulders. The height is measured in hands. A Paint usually is 14.2 to 16 hands tall. One hand equals 4 inches (10 centimeters).

Personality

Paints are calm. They often stay calm even in unfamiliar surroundings. Their personalities make them excellent horses for children.

Paints also are intelligent. People have success training Paints for almost any activity.

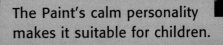

The Paint's calm personality makes it suitable for children.

Expressive eyes

Finely muscled neck

Broad chest

Muscular hindquarters

Strong legs

Chapter 3

Western Pleasure Winners

The Paint's athletic build allows it to perform well at competitions. Paint owners and their horses compete at thousands of horse shows each year.

Horse Shows

Many horse shows are local or regional. Paints often compete against other breeds of horses at these shows. Some shows are recognized by the APHA. Only registered Paints can participate in these shows.

Learn about:
- ★ Paint horse shows
- ★ Western saddles
- ★ Training Paints

Many Paints compete in the
Western pleasure class at shows.

Western pleasure Paints must carry their head level and move slowly.

Shows have several events called classes. Classes are offered for both youth and adults. People ride Paints in many classes. In halter classes, competitors lead their horses. Horses are judged on their physical features in halter classes.

Western Pleasure

The Paint's eye-catching looks and relaxed personality make it a tough competitor in the Western pleasure class. In this class, riders ask their horses to perform three gaits. These gaits are the walk, the jog, and the lope.

Horses are judged according to their performance in the class. Each gait should be slow and smooth. Consistency is important in the Western pleasure class. Horses should keep their head in about the same position throughout the class. Horses also should perform each gait at the same pace.

Horses must respond well to their riders in the Western pleasure class. They should quickly and calmly go from one gait to another.

Western Tack and Clothing

Competitors in the Western pleasure class use Western equipment, or tack. They use Western saddles. These large, sturdy saddles have a saddle horn. Some people use Western saddles that are decorated with silver in shows.

Western clothing is needed for the Western pleasure class. Competitors wear long-sleeved shirts, belts, cowboy hats, cowboy boots, and long pants. Many competitors wear chaps. These leather leggings fit over riders' pants.

Western Pleasure Training

Paints that are at least 2 years old usually are ready to be ridden. At first, trainers often attach a horse to a long rope called a longe line. The horses learn to respond to commands while moving in a circle around the trainer.

Soon, trainers fit a horse with a saddle and a bridle. A bridle includes straps that fit around a horse's head. It also has a metal bit that fits in the horse's mouth. Straps called reins lead from the bit to the rider.

People training horses for Western pleasure must ride often. They teach their horses to move slowly at each gait. The horses learn to bring their hind legs well underneath their bodies while moving. People also teach their horses to back up smoothly.

Charlie Cole

Charlie Cole of Pilot Point, Texas, is one of the most successful Paint competitors. Cole was the high point exhibitor at the World Championship Paint Horse Show in 2002, 2003, and 2004. He has won world and reserve championships in Western riding, trail, and pleasure driving. Cole has finished in the top 10 in several other events.

Chapter 4

Paints in Action

Some people show Paints at national or international levels. Each June, the APHA holds the World Championship Paint Horse Show in Fort Worth, Texas. People can show only Paints that are registered with the APHA at this show. The show includes about 160 classes and lasts for two weeks. The APHA gives out about $200,000 in prize money at the show. About 2,000 Paints compete there each year.

Learn about:
- ★ Awards
- ★ Rodeo events
- ★ Paint racing

Paints often show their ranching skills at competitions.

Rodeos and Racing

Many Paints compete in events other than horse shows. Some Paints compete at rodeos. Rodeo events include calf roping and barrel racing. In calf roping, riders chase a calf and use a rope to catch it. They then get off the horse and tie down the calf. In barrel racing,

Paint horses that race are in top physical condition.

riders complete a pattern around three barrels. They try to do the pattern in the least amount of time without knocking down the barrels.

Paints' powerful hindquarters give them racing ability. The APHA has a racing program for registered Paints. In 2003, APHA races were held in 15 states.

Owning a Paint

Owning a Paint is rewarding, but it also is a big responsibility. Paints and other horses need a great deal of care. They need food, water, shelter, and exercise. Many people keep their Paints at their farms. Other owners pay to have their horses stay at another person's farm or stable.

Hundreds of years ago, a spotted horse from Europe led to the start of a new breed. Today, the number of Paints in North America continues to soar. The colorful spotted horses will keep turning heads both in and out of the show ring.

Fast Facts:
The American Paint Horse

Name: During the 1800s and 1900s, people had many names for early ancestors of Paints. People called them piebalds, skewbalds, and pintos.

History: In 1519, Spanish explorer Hernán Cortés brought a spotted horse to North America. The horse mated with other horses. The offspring of these horses were early relatives of today's Paints.

Height: Paints are 14.2 to 16 hands (about 5 feet or 1.5 meters) tall at the withers. Each hand equals 4 inches (10 centimeters).

Weight: 1,000 to 1,200 pounds (450 to 540 kilograms)

Colors: Most Paints have a solid body color and at least one white spot. Black, bay, brown, chestnut, and buckskin are common coat colors.

Features: muscular body frame; broad chest; flat forehead; small, pointed ears; strong legs; powerful hindquarters

Personality: calm, intelligent, cooperative

Abilities: Many people ride Paints in Western classes at horse shows. Paints also are good horses for rodeos, trail riding, and racing.

Life span: about 25 to 30 years

Glossary

bit (BIT)—the metal mouthpiece of the bridle

bridle (BRYE-duhl)—the straps that fit around a horse's head and connect to a bit to control a horse while riding

camouflage (KAM-uh-flahzh)—coloring that makes people, animals, or objects look like their surroundings

chaps (SHAPS)—leather leggings that fit over pants; chaps protect the legs of riders on horseback.

gait (GATE)—the manner in which a horse moves; gaits include the walk, jog, and lope.

longe line (LUNJ LINE)—a long rope that attaches to a horse; horses on a longe line are taught to move in a circle around the trainer while responding to verbal commands.

mate (MAYT)—to join together to produce young

registry (REH-juh-stree)—an organization that keeps track of the ancestry for horses of a certain breed

Read More

Barnes, Julia. *101 Facts about Horses and Ponies.* 101 Facts about Pets. Milwaukee: Gareth Stevens, 2002.

Lomberg, Michelle. *Caring for Your Horse.* Caring for Your Pet. New York: Weigl Publishers, 2004.

Murray, Julie. *Pinto Horses.* Animal Kingdom. Edina, Minn.: Abdo, 2003.

Internet Sites

FactHound offers a safe, fun way to find Internet sites related to this book. All of the sites on FactHound have been researched by our staff.

Here's how:

1. Visit *www.facthound.com*
2. Type in this special code **0736837639** for age-appropriate sites. Or enter a search word related to this book for a more general search.
3. Click on the **Fetch It** button.

FactHound will fetch the best sites for you!

Index